I Tip
My Hat

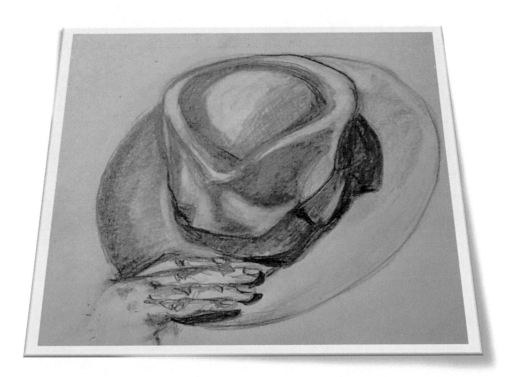

A GRANDDAUGHTER REMINISCES

CATHY LINDA BROOKS

Archway Publishing books may be ordered through booksellers or by contacting:

Archway Publishing
1663 Liberty Drive
Bloomington, IN 47403
www.archwaypublishing.com
844-669-3957

ISBN: 978-1-6657-5412-5 (sc)
ISBN: 978-1-6657-5414-9 (hc)
ISBN: 978-1-6657-5413-2 (e)

Library of Congress Control Number: 2023923422

Print information available on the last page.

Archway Publishing rev. date: 01/30/2024

I Tip My Hat:
A Granddaughter Reminisces

Cathy Linda Brooks

Delphine Brooks Baldon
Illustrator,
Research Collaborator

July 23, 2021
Dallas, Texas

Dedication

This book is dedicated to the memories of three remarkable men. The first is James Brooks, my paternal grandfather, who was born July 14, 1879 in Clarksville, Virginia. The second is my grandfather's grandfather-in-law David Singleton who fought in the Union Army from 1863 - 1865 and registered to vote in 1869. The third is Jeff Jeter, my Great-Aunt Pearl Jeter's nephew-in-law. (Pearl Jeter was my grandfather's sister-in-law.) Jeff Jeter refused to move to the back of the bus when he returned home after serving in World War II. With his gun by his side, he maintained his seat.

Table of Contents

| S | 51 | **U.S.C.T.** |

David Singleton

Priv., Capt. Munn's Co., 1 Reg't Miss. Inf., A. D.*

Age 22 years.

Appears on

Company Muster-in Roll

of the organization named above. Roll dated

Millikens Bend, La., July 28, 1863.

Muster-in to date July 28, 1863.

Joined for duty and enrolled:

When July 18, 1863.

Where Canton, Miss.

Period 3 years.

Remarks :

*This organization subsequently became Co. D, 51 Reg't U. S. Colored Infantry.

Book mark :

(356) Copyist.

David Singleton

Voter Registration, Sabine County

Texas, Voter Registration Lists, 1867-1869

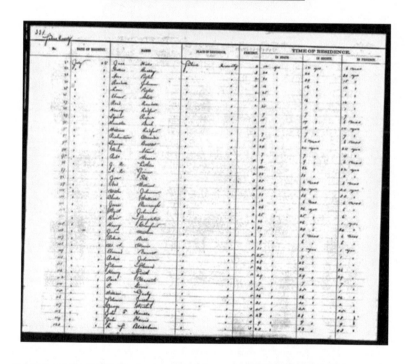

May 28, 2016

Dear Beloved Brooks' Sons and Daughters,

I wanted to give you a gift that delighted me so in the discovery. It is a gift that is both tangible and abstract. I am presenting copies of Grandfather James Brooks' World War I and World War II Draft Registration Cards.

My father, Isaiah Brooks, has regaled us with stories of my grandfather's patriotism and respect for the military - officers in particular. Seeing the images of these draft cards deepened my appreciation of what my grandfather felt. Initially, I mistakenly thought that I had discovered war service records. I thought that must be why Grandfather revered the military so. For many years, I believed that my grandfather who was born during the Reconstruction Era, had a reverence for the military because of the ever present troops that he would have been exposed to in the Deep South. Grandfather's reason for loving the military was his own, but I am free to romanticize his patriotism as much as I choose.

These draft card images also helped me to solidify the image - for me - of a wise man who wrote to the United States Military to request that his second son be discharged from the army, because my grandfather was very ill. Grandfather needed the unmarried James Brooks, Jr. to be present to assume Grandfather's role as head of the family.

These records are so beloved to me, because they contain my grandfather's signature. Nothing except one's reputation is more personal. They also contain, I believe his exact birth date. I also believe that they contain his birth city and state - Clarksville, Virginia.

My grandfather was very intelligent and - of course what follows is my interpretation many years after the fact with no direct knowledge of the truth - would know that the information in these records would only be used for the intended purpose. That purpose would be to identify men who could possibly be called to fight for the country that Grandfather loved.

I thank my sisters Delphine and Yvette - Delphine who introduced me to our family history and my sister Yvette who remembers many details about family members. I also want to thank Aunt Evelyn, the family historian.

I love you all, none more than my own mother and father, Isaiah and Jimmie Brooks. Because of my father's stories, I have a visual image of my grandfather tipping his hat to soldiers and my father standing by his side that will never disappear.

I wanted to help preserve the gift that my grandfather gave us all. There was always tangible evidence of Grandfather's love, but my brilliant grandfather would also want us to guard our intellects and to continue to seek knowledge about all things.

With a love that will never end,
Cathy Linda Brooks

James Brooks

World War I Draft Registration Card

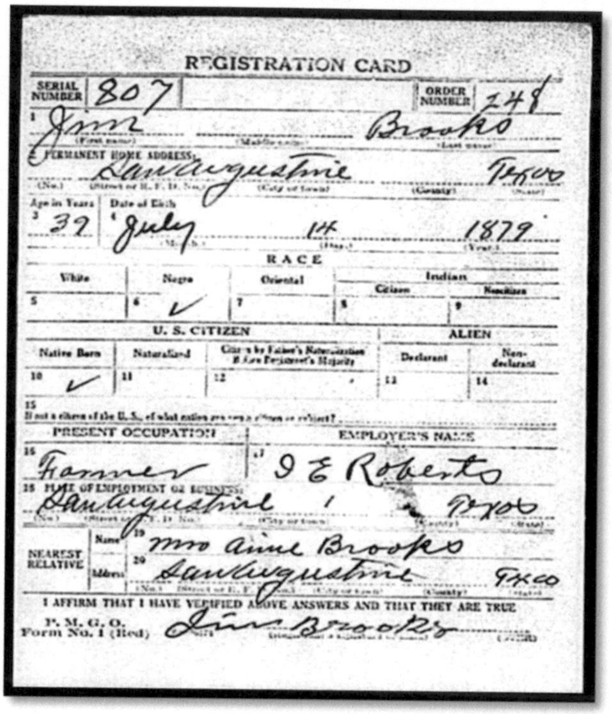

REGISTRATION CARD

SERIAL NUMBER 807 ORDER NUMBER 248

1 Jim Brooks
(First name) (Middle name) (Last name)

2 PERMANENT HOME ADDRESS:
San Augustine Texas
(No.) (Street or R. F. D. No.) (City or town) (County) (State)

Age in Years 3 39 Date of Birth 4 July 14 1879
(Month.) (Day.) (Year.)

RACE

White	Negro	Oriental	Indian Citizen	Indian Noncitizen
5	6 ✓	7	8	9

U. S. CITIZEN / ALIEN

Native Born	Naturalized	Citizen by Father's Naturalization Before Registrant's Majority	Declarant	Non-declarant
10 ✓	11	12	13	14

15 If not a citizen of the U. S., of what nation are you a citizen or subject?

PRESENT OCCUPATION 16 Farmer
EMPLOYER'S NAME 17 I E Roberts

18 PLACE OF EMPLOYMENT OR BUSINESS:
San Augustine Texas
(No.) (Street or R. F. D. No.) (City or town) (County) (State)

NEAREST RELATIVE Name 19 Mrs Anne Brooks
Address 20 San Augustine Texas

I AFFIRM THAT I HAVE VERIFIED ABOVE ANSWERS AND THAT THEY ARE TRUE

P. M. G. O. Form No. 1 (Red) Jim Brooks
(Registrant's signature or mark)

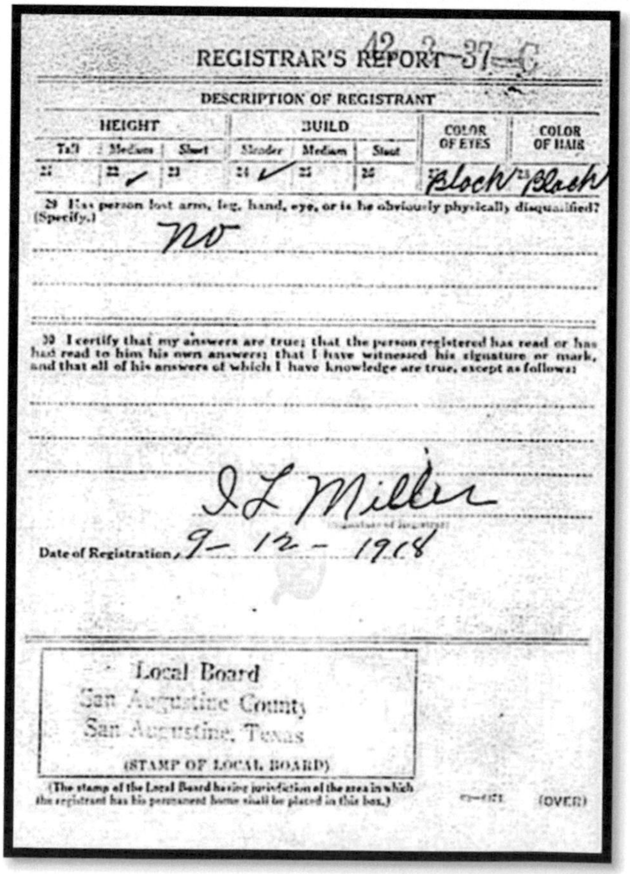

REGISTRAR'S REPORT 42-3-37-C

DESCRIPTION OF REGISTRANT

HEIGHT Tall	Medium	Short	BUILD Slender	Medium	Stout	COLOR OF EYES	COLOR OF HAIR
21	22 ✓	23	24 ✓	25	26	Black	Black

29 Has person lost arm, leg, hand, eye, or is he obviously physically disqualified? (Specify.)
No

30 I certify that my answers are true; that the person registered has read or has had read to him his own answers; that I have witnessed his signature or mark, and that all of his answers of which I have knowledge are true, except as follows:

I L Miller
(Signature of registrar)

Date of Registration 9-12-1918

Local Board
San Augustine County
San Augustine, Texas

(STAMP OF LOCAL BOARD)

(The stamp of the Local Board having jurisdiction of the area in which the registrant has his permanent home shall be placed in this box.)

(OVER)

World War II Draft Registration Card

I Tip My Hat: A Granddaughter Reminisces

This photographic history is being presented to my father Isaiah Brooks and his twin brother Isaac Brooks on July 23, 2021, my birthday. Daddy and Uncle Isaac have always led and served their families with valor and distinction. I owe a special debt of gratitude to my family who contributed the photographs for this book.

"Before I became a Christian, I only tipped my hat to pretty women and military officers," My father Isaiah Brooks says my Grandfather James Brooks often told his family.

Grandfather, however, did not just stand around tipping his hat.

Grandfather took two nine-year-old boys and an eleven-year-old girl and cultivated a farm in 1944. This was something that others thought would be an impossible task for "an old man and two little boys," declared Uncle Isaac. Grandfather gave lectures about his farming techniques to college students from nearby Marshall, Texas who visited his farm to learn more about agricultural practices. Grandfather did not mind embellishing his practices to make a good story for the young "chaps", his daughter – the eleven-year-old - Evelyn Maude Brooks McCray recalled.

Grandfather loved regaling people with his stories, but he also loved hunting and his dogs. He could distinguish each of his dogs from each other just by listening to their barking, Daddy said. Daddy and Uncle Isaac would follow him into the woods at night, but they never had their father's affinity for hunting or for dogs. (Daddy shot one rabbit with a 44-Rifle that he and Uncle Isaac purchased together.) Grandfather carried an axe and a rifle into the woods to hunt. Grandfather would chop down a bough from a tree and one of the dogs would then "tree" the raccoon. Grandfather would call out the name of the dog who was successful as soon as the barking commenced.

Grandfather also read the Bible during the week and a minister named Isaac Strong, who could not read would deliver sermons and sing. My grandfather was remarkable. He was born two years after the end of Reconstruction and had graduated from high school. When my sisters, and nieces, and I visited his birthplace, Clarksville, Virginia, we learned that there were many schools and universities there, which was the likely reason that he had received a formal education. The accomplishment becomes even more remarkable when one considers that Clarksville is 107 miles from Richmond, the Capital of the Confederacy.

This book, a compilation of military photographs, is a way for Grandfather's descendants and family members to "tip" their hats to him. The book contains pictures or draft records belonging to him, his progeny, his grandfather-in-law, and his wife's nephew-in-law once removed.

Daddy and Uncle Isaac share their father's sentiment for pretty women. The way the brothers have never shied away from hard work has been a metaphorical tipping of their hats to their father's legacy.

Twins and Wives

Isaiah and Jimmie Brooks   Isaac and Cecelia Brooks

Photo Gallery

James (Son) Brooks

United States Army: World War II and the Aftermath
Son of Patriarch James Brooks

James Brooks' Draft Registration Card

FORM APPROVED
Budget Bureau No. 33–R012–42

REGISTRATION CARD (Men born on or after July 1, 1924, and on or before December 31, 1924)
(Also for the registration of men as they reach the 18th anniversary of the date of their birth on or after January 1, 1943.)

SERIAL NUMBER W 322

1. NAME (Print)
James (NONE) Brooks Jr.
(First) (Middle) (Last)

ORDER NUMBER 11910

2. PLACE OF RESIDENCE (Print)
RT 1 Box 29 L   DeBerry   Texas
(Number and street) (Town, township, village, or city) (County) (State)

[THE PLACE OF RESIDENCE GIVEN ON LINE 2 ABOVE WILL DETERMINE LOCAL BOARD
JURISDICTION; LINE 2 OF REGISTRATION CERTIFICATE WILL BE IDENTICAL]

3. MAILING ADDRESS
Same
(Mailing address if other than place indicated on line 2. If same, insert word same)

4. TELEPHONE
(Exchange) (Number)

5. AGE IN YEARS 18
DATE OF BIRTH
March 24 1926
(Mo.) (Day) (Yr.)

6. PLACE OF BIRTH
Panola Co
(Town or county)
Texas
(State or country)

7. NAME AND ADDRESS OF PERSON WHO WILL ALWAYS KNOW YOUR ADDRESS
Jim Brooks RT 1 Bx 29 L DeBerry Tex.

8. EMPLOYER'S NAME AND ADDRESS
Silas Hudson R1 DeBerry Texas

9. PLACE OF EMPLOYMENT OR BUSINESS
RT 1   DeBerry Panol Texas
(Number and street or R. F. D. number) (Town) (County) (State)

I AFFIRM THAT I HAVE VERIFIED ABOVE ANSWERS AND THAT THEY ARE TRUE.

DSS Form 1 (Rev. 11–16–42)   c16—21630-4   (OVER)   JAMES BROOKS JR
(Registrant's signature)

REGISTRAR'S REPORT
DESCRIPTION OF REGISTRANT

RACE		HEIGHT (Approx.)	WEIGHT (Approx.)	COMPLEXION	
White		5'11"	180	Sallow	
		EYES	HAIR	Light	
Negro	✓	Blue	Blonde	Ruddy	
Indian		Gray	Red	Dark	
		Hazel	Brown	Freckled	
Filipino		Brown ✓	Black ✓	Light brown	
Japanese		Black	Gray	Dark brown	✓
Other Oriental			Bald	Black	

Other obvious physical characteristics that will aid in identification
Scar on rt elbow

I certify that my answers are true; that the person registered has read or has had
read to him his own answers; that I have witnessed his signature or mark and that
all of his answers of which I have knowledge are true, except as follows:

BPKyle
(Signature of registrar)

Registrar for Local Board 1 Panola Texas
(Number) (State)

Date of registration Mar. 18–44

LOCAL BOARD
1st Nat'l Bank Bldg.
CARTHAGE, TEXAS
PANOLA COUNTY

(The stamp of the Local Board having jurisdiction of the registrant
shall be placed in the above space)

U. S. GOVERNMENT PRINTING OFFICE   16o—21630-1

Frank Fite

United States Army: February 25, 1943 - January 13, 1946
April 8, 1948 – February 13, 1950
Son-in-law of Patriarch James Brooks

John Baldon

Specialist E4 Retail United States Army: October 21, 1966 – August 26, 1968
Buffalo Soldier Regiment
Grandson-in-law of Patriarch James Brooks
Son-in-law of Isaiah Brooks

Melvin Thomas Roberson, Jr.

Medic United States Army: July 23, 1970 – April 21, 1972
Grandson of Patriarch James Brooks
Son of Emma Lee Brooks Roberson

James (Sonny) Brooks

Specialist E4 Jet Mechanic United States Navy: 1971-1975
Grandson of Patriarch James Brooks
Son of James Brooks

Ike Sims

Specialist E4 United States Army: 1972-1976
Grandson of Patriarch James Brooks
Son of Evelyn Brooks Sims McCray

Jeffrey Brooks

Specialist E4 United States Army: 1980-1985
Grandson of Patriarch James Brooks
Son of James Brooks

Delores Brooks Blankumsee

Specialist E4 United States Army: 1980-1987
Granddaughter of Patriarch James Brooks
Daughter of James Brooks

Gloria Brooks Hawkins

Sergeant United States Air Force: 1981–1988
Granddaughter of Patriarch James Brooks
Daughter of James Brooks

Isaac Kevin Brooks

Specialist E4 United States Army: 1986-1994
Grandson of Patriarch James Brooks
Son of Isaac Brooks

Otis (Tom) Amy

Specialist E4 United States Army: 1992-1995
Great-grandson of Patriarch James Brooks
Grandson of Calvin Ross (Bear) Brooks
Son of Calvin Jean (Patsy) Brooks Amy

Kelly Grogan

United States Air Force: 2009 – 2015
Great-great-grandson of Patriarch James Brooks
Great-grandson of Evelyn Brooks Sims McCray
Grandson of Deon Sims Chisum
Son of Dawana Booker

Ericke Washington

Specialist E3 United States Army: 2012-2015
Great-great-grandson of Patriarch James Brooks
Great-grandson of Evelyn Brooks Sims McCray
Grandson of Ike Sims
Son of Ikeinia Simone Sims

Danielle Norris

Specialist E4 ATO United States Navy: 2012-2020
Great-granddaughter of Patriarch James Brooks
Granddaughter of Isaac Brooks
Daughter of Angela (Angel) Brooks Norris

Matthew Norris

Specialist E5 SW2 United States Navy: 2012-Present
Great-grandson of Patriarch James Brooks
Grandson of Isaac Brooks
Son of Angela Brooks Norris

Marquis Stevens

Specialist E4 United States Navy: Honorable Discharge 2016
Great-great grandson of Patriarch James Brooks
Great-grandson of Evelyn Brooks Sims McCray
Grandson of Melanie Renee McMillan
Son of Tamia Hairell

Christian Allison

E5 Army National Guard: 2016-2020
Great-great-grandson of Patriarch James Brooks
Great-grandson of Betty Ann Brooks
Grandson of Linda (Lucy) Brooks Williams
Son of Christie Glenn-Moore

Talil Sims

United States Navy: 2017 – Present
Great-great-grandson of Patriarch James Brooks
Great-grandson of Evelyn Brooks Sims McCray
Grandson of Ike Sims
Son of Ikeinia Simone Sims

Ashton Jamison

United States Marines: Present
Great-great-grandson of Patriarch James Brooks
Great-grandson of Evelyn Brooks Sims McCray
Grandson of Melanie Renee McMillan
Son of Ashley Hairell

Alexandria Olivia Amy

Hospital Corpsman Third Class United States Navy: Present
Great-great-granddaughter of Patriarch James Brooks
Great-granddaughter of Calvin Ross Brooks
Granddaughter of Calvin Jean Brooks Amy
Daughter of Otis Amy

Family Profiles

Patriarch James Brooks (July 14, 1879 – January 24, 1948)
And Matriarch Annie Singleton Brooks (August 23, 1898 – 1951)
Married November 7, 1917

I.   *Daughter* Jessie Lee (Cootie) Brooks
     (December 23, 1920 - February 25, 2009)

II. *Son* Calvin Ross (Bear) Brooks (March 10, 1924 – March 21, 2000)
     A. *Great-grandson* Otis Amy: Specialist E4 United States Army
     B. *Great-great-granddaughter* Alexandria Olivia Amy: Hospital Corpsman Third Class United States Navy

III. *Son* James Brooks: United States Army
     (March 12, 1926 - September 26, 2010)
     A. *Grandson* James Brooks: Specialist E4 Jet Mechanic United States Navy
     B. *Granddaughter* Gloria Brooks Hawkins: Sergeant United States Air Force
     C. *Grandson* Jeffrey Brooks: Specialist E4 United States Army
     D. *Granddaughter* Delores Brooks Blankumsee: Specialist E4 United States Army

IV. *Daughter* Emma Lee Brooks Roberson (January 20, 1930 – April 24, 1951)
     Grandson Melvin Thomas Roberson, Jr: United States Army

V.   *Daughter* Evelyn Brooks Sims McCray (September 18, 1932 - Present)
     A. *Grandson* Ike Sims: Specialist E4 United States Army
     B. *Great-great-grandson* Kelly Grogan: United States Air Force
     C. *Great-great-grandson* Ericke Washington: Specialist E3 United States Army
     D. Great-great-grandson Marquis Stevens: Specialist E4 United States Navy
     E. Great-great-grandson Talil Sims: United States Navy
     F. *Great-great-grandson* Ashton Jamison: United States Marines

VI. *Son* Isaac Brooks (January 27, 1935 - Present)
     A. *Grandson* Isaac Kevin Brooks: Specialist E4 United States Army
     B. *Great-granddaughter* Danielle Norris: Specialist E4 ATO United States Navy
     C. *Great-grandson* Matthew Norris: Specialist E5 SW2 United States Navy

VII. *Son* Isaiah Brooks (January 27, 1935 – Present)
     Grandson-in-law John Baldon: Specialist United States Army

VIII. *Daughter* Betty Ann Brooks (October 23,1938 – May 9, 1963)
     Great-great-grandson Christian Allison: Specialist E5 Army National Guard

IX. *Baby Daughter* Annie Pearl

X.   *Daughter* Alice Pearl Brooks Fite (July 11, 1944 – Present)
     Son-in-law Frank Fite, Sr.: United States Army

Jeff Jeter's Draft Registration Card

June 16, 2021

Enlisting in the American Civil War was a way for David Singleton, my great-great-grandfather, and other men of African descent to assert their voices and give rise to a new form of protest: war itself. While men of African descent had fought and died in other wars in the United States from its beginnings, men of African descent enlisted in the Civil War to obtain liberty and citizenship and the right to define who they were against an entrenched backdrop of racism in the nation. Fighting for the dignity of all people of African descent was a resounding shout that echoed across the nation. Protests ultimately are the voices that signal the beginning of battles that eventually have to be won in the consciences of society, judicial, and legislative bodies. That was true of the men of African descent's battles during the Civil War, but it was a volley that set the stage to dismantle some forms of legal oppression and made it impossible to continue to silence the voices of men of African descent. David Singleton, who fought in the American Civil War from 1863 - 1865, was registered to vote July 26, 1869 in Sabine County, Texas.

David Singleton's Military Service Rolls

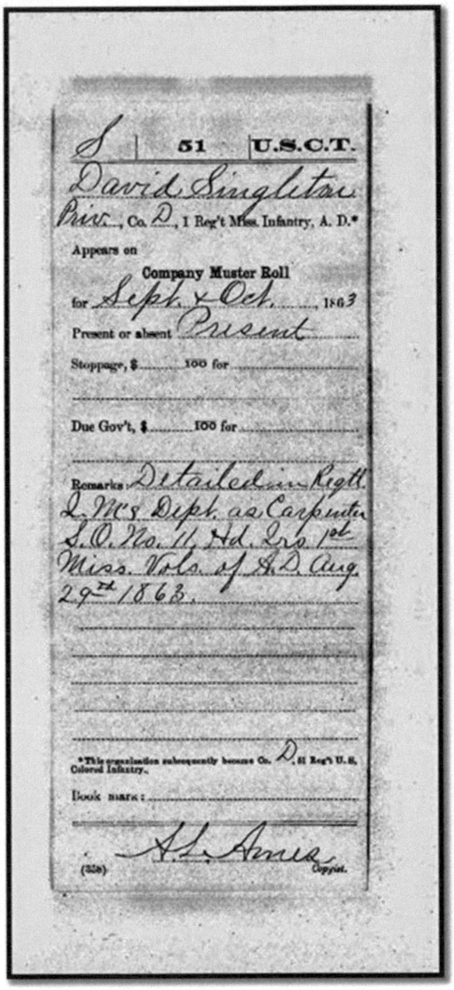

S | 51 | U.S.C.T.

David Singletan

Priv., Co. D, 1 Reg't Miss. Infantry, A. D.*

Appears on

Company Muster Roll

for Sept. & Oct., 1863

Present or absent Present

Stoppage, $...... 100 for ......

Due Gov't, $...... 100 for ......

Remarks: Detailed in Regtl. Q. M's Dept. as Carpenter S. O. No. 11, Hd. Qrs. 1st Miss. Vols. of A. D. Aug. 29th 1863.

*This organization subsequently became Co. D, 51 Reg't U. S. Colored Infantry.

Book mark: ......

A. L. Ames
Copyist.

(358)

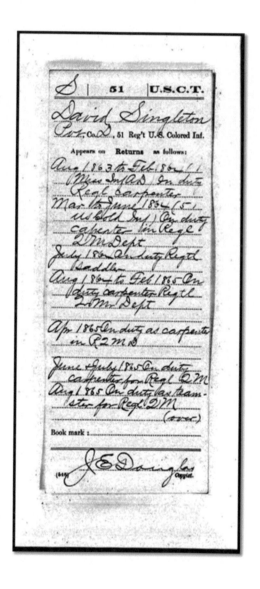

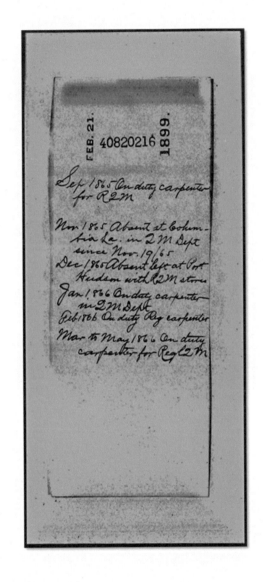

Sep 1865 On duty carpenter
for R2M

Nov 1865 Absent at Colum-
bia La. in 2 M Dept
since Nov. 19/65

Dec 1865 Absent left at Port
Hudson with R2M stores

Jan 1866 On duty carpenter
in 2 M Dept

Feb 1866 On duty Reg carpenter

Mar to May 1866 On duty
carpenter for Regl 2 M

| S | 51 | U.S.C.T. |

David Singleton

Prt , Co. A , 51 Reg't U. S. Col'd Infantry.

Appears on **Co. Muster-out Roll**, dated

Baton Rouge, La. June 16, 186 6.

Muster-out to date _June 16_ 186 6.

Last paid to _Dec. 31,_ 186 5.

Clothing account:

Last settled _____, 186 ; drawn since $ ____ 100

Due soldier $ 28 75 ; due U. S. $ ____ 100

Am't for cloth'g in kind or money adv'd $ ____ 100

Due U. S. for arms, equipments, &c., $ ____ 95/100

Bounty paid $ ____ 100 ; due $ ____ 100

Remarks _found at original_
organization.
Prop S. Havens A 1

Book mark : _____

(561)   Jno B Bell Jr

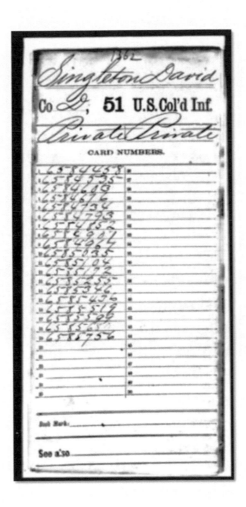

Granddaughters Cathy Linda Brooks
and Delphine Brooks Baldon -wearing the hat -
are proud to present this photographic
history to their father Isaiah Brooks and
his twin brother Isaac Brooks.
Ironically, the sisters are pictured in front of
George Washington's Mount Vernon
Estate in February 2016.

Printed in the United States
by Baker & Taylor Publisher Services